Life, Loss & Love

– Poems of Prayer and Promise –

Laurie Luongo
– & –
Lucas E. Angelastro

Contact Laurie Luongo at LaurieLauthor@gmail.com

ISBN 978-1-949085-27-3

Cover design by Kari Ley, Leyout Solutions

CKBooks Publishing
PO Box 214
New Glarus, WI
53574
Ckbookspublishing.com

Dedication

This book of poetry represents more than 20 years of life, love and loss. It is dedicated first to Lucas Angelastro, my best friend for close to forty years. We started the writings in 1970 and continued through the late 1990's. Luke was gifted in so many ways, and his poems, stories and songs are one of the creative aspects I loved about him. Luke showed me how to live and love. He was so genuine and giving. He had high expectations for everything that he did and he accomplished so many different things. I am honored and humbled to call him the best friend I ever had and I miss him for those reasons and so many more. He was taken from the world way too soon at the age of 50

I also dedicate this work to my sister Nicole Luongo, the baby of eleven in my family. Nicole was born 47 years ago with cerebral palsy, which is the most common childhood disability worldwide yet receives scant attention or media coverage. Seventeen million children and adults live with CP. Nicole has been an ardent CP advocate for years. She was the first person ever in 2019 to get buildings, bridges and landmarks all over the world to light up in green (CP's color) for both National Cerebral Palsy Day (observed each March) and World Cerebral Palsy Day (observed in October). She was on a mission to achieve national media attention for CP awareness and for CP to be recognized globally as with other diseases and illnesses like breast cancer and autism among others. Nicole wrote "Naked Desires," a poetry book in 2003. She is a published author and blogger with a verified Facebook page.

To my partner, Lee Weiss, who is legally blind. I met Lee when he had limited vision and was in constant amazement at what he could do without sight. An avid fisherman since childhood, Lee does everything except drive the boat. When he goes out on the lake or on the ocean, his fellow fishermen are stunned to witness his fishing acumen, from locating the correct rod to reeling in the biggest catch. Lee was in the meat business for years following in his grandfather's and fathers' foot-steps. He has the uncanny ability when he asks how one would like their steak cooked, to prepare it exactly as requested. He has been a business owner and entrepreneur while learning computer and other assistive skills through voice over technology.

Lucas, Nicole, Lee and millions of others with the word "disabled" attached to their name, are doing amazing things and changing the world! This is for all of them.

Introduction

Over fifty years ago, me and my best friend from grade school, talked about one day publishing a book of poems. Lukey, as he was affectionately called, was quite proficient at writing ~ letters, poetry and song. I was enamored with poetry as a hopeless romantic at the time. So, each of us wrote, scribbled and typed our works and kept them compiled in our separate yellow manila envelopes.

Luke died in 2002 at age 50. He had become a paraplegic as a teenager – we had already graduated from St. Bernadette's Catholic school. After two years in a rehabilitation facility in northern Florida, he returned home where his parents welcomed him like a new-born infant. Betty, his mom, who never worked outside the home, was the penultimate caregiver. Big Luke, who had arms of steel, built a room onto the house that accommodated Lukey's wheelchair and water bed, which he so enjoyed. Big Luke was a high school vocational education teacher for many years. He also sang professionally in clubs throughout Florida under the name Vic Martone. After retiring from teaching, he opened a moving company business and Lukey worked the phones and did the paperwork to assist his dad. He often told me funny stories of peoples' moves that elicited laughter until we cried.

In 1976, I drove us to Miami in my green VW beetle to see Peter Frampton live and in concert. It was a hot and humid summer day in the outdoor arena, and we had a wonderful time. Still I can hear "Baby I love Your Way," which was my favorite Frampton song then and now. One year, I cannot recall when, we also went to see George Carlin in concert. Lukey loved to hear Carlin's rendition of the "Seven Dirty Words," which always cracked him up.

I visited the Angelastro home very often, including on my trips to Florida long after I graduated from the University of Florida. In fact, one jaunt included driving to UF with Lukey with wheelchair in tow so he could visit the campus. We did a lot of things together, and he was a champ. Never in my almost forty years of friendship with him did I ever hear him complain or bemoan the fact that he was a paraplegic. He did things that able-bodied people do not even attempt. Lukey loved to fish, to write and play the guitar. He was a disability advocate long before it became a cause that many avow. At one point, he lived on his own and had a specially-equipped van that he maneuvered in and out of like a pro. He was as independent as one could be, given his condition.

Lukey's immediate family members are all gone now ~ his maternal grandma, who lived with them, his dad, Big Luke, his only sibling, Lisa, and dear Betty. I have such fond memories of all of them and the many chats and discussions we had at their kitchen table.

As the years passed, I moved all over the country for my jobs in the hotel industry. Packed boxes, often not opened, traveled with me from state to state. One day I would go through them when I had time. After Lukey passed away, his mom sent me a few packages that included his poems, letters and songs. I stored them amongst the many boxes of old things that I would get to one day. That day came in 2019 when I was no longer gainfully employed and in my second career as a writer.

After I wrote my first book, I started on the journey of going through those boxes. There I found that old, tattered manila envelope containing the many poems written decades ago. I decided then and there, as a tribute to Luke, to publish them. So, here is *Life, Loss and Love ~ Poems of Prayer and Promise*. It is a labor of love to him, for him and for all those who yearn for the special friendship that Luke and I shared. "Here's looking at you, kid."

For

RDJ

Disappointment
From Start To End

At first I thought you loved me
When I gave you my high school ring
And when you said you loved me
I gave you everything.

Then later on we married
I still remember while
Together as one
We walked down the aisle.

I gave you a home and happiness
And so I don't know why
You left me, one lonely man
And went to that honkey-tonk guy.

I still look at your picture
Hanging on the wall
But I still don't understand
Why you fell for it all

But maybe they'll be others
Who will love me true
And I hope that my next lover
Doesn't do the things you do.

Anyway I hope you're happy
now
With your fancy city life.
But I'll always remember you
As my lover and my wife

And when the Lord calls me
For when my life is through
I'll still ask Him
To save a place for you

L.E.A.

i like cold winter nights
when the wind is blowing
hot summer days when it's not

i like french perfume
anything cotton
soft things
and endings to good movies

i like pretty things
the color yellow
big eyes and
boys with long lashes

i like the first day of spring
a summer vacation
the fall term of school
and the feeling of winter

i like a good sense of humor
high cheek bones
guy with beards
and foreign countries

i like seeing the sun rise
watching it set
seagulls and
wild flowers

i like "real" people
happy children
sharing with others
and joy

i like sitting
near the window on a DC-10
a rainbow in the sky
blue clouds
and a full moon

i like the word love
breathing the fresh air
peaceful moments
and i especially like
thinking . . .
about these things i like

L.L.

On Thinking of the World

Here I sit neath this mighty oak
Towering above me as if I were
From it's very womb as it
Is old, and it's leafy boughs.
Have had ice cover them for
Many winters.
And they have silently whispered
Their mysterious song when
The summer breeze enticed them
To do so.
And wise? Ah, but this tree
Seems very wise, as it's
Stately figure adorns the open
Field like a fly on a white
Tablecloth.
It's mighty limbs bend and
Creak, though they are always

Protecting the nesting birds, and
A lone Red squirrel that heard
Acorns in a hollow of the tree
Trunk.
As I sit here, young, much younger
Than the tree against which I lean,
I think How old are you, tree?
How many decades have you been
Standing here, once a mere acorn,
But now look at the size of you.
You are king of your domain!
All around and about you
Look toward you for comfort
And advice, and they seek to .
Have your wisdom.
Oh yeah, I remember several
Summers ago, when lightning
Struck you half dead, crippling
Thru of your mightiest boughs,
Yes, there they are over there, But
They are still a part of you,
And you continue to provide food
And shelter for even the lowly termites.
But still, as I ponder your age,
I can't help wonder how many
Other lads have done the same
as I am doing now; and perhaps my
Children will sit on your grassy,
Sloping roots and ask you
Questions out loud, and you will
Hear them, but, mighty oak, will
You ever answer them, or anyone at all?   *L.E.A.*

A Different Kind of Chair

I am bound, yes, to this clinking clattering chrome plated collec-
tion
Of nuts, bolts, and whatever else compresses this
Eternal, four wheeled rolling prison I call transportation.
Bound, yes; but certainly, God knows,
By no given choice of my own.

One may take philosophy in hand and ask, "Don't you loathe it?
"Don't you begrudge the wretched chair? Do you long and ache to
"Stretch your limbs...to get up, and smash the rattling thing to the
ground?"

But for what purpose?

Surely I loathe it. Of course I begrudge it.
But to beat it and break it...to smash it irreparably?
Why?
Let us think of the thing for a moment: I work from it,
I learn from it, I eat from it, I relax in it.
And, when all of my work is done, and my time is my own,
I indulge myself in my hobbies from it. The chair is a part of
Me. An inanimate, yet very essential part of me,
And of my existence.

Should I, by some miracle of God be able to leap from the chair,
Surely there is someone, somewhere, whose feet can rest upon
The weathered, gray foot pedals.

To seek revenge, or annihilation of the chair
Would, no doubt, draw a frown from many; and most
Certainly a look of disgust from God.

There is a reason, though I have never fully understood

why. I seek not to banish this chair from my life,
But to learn from it...to work with it, not against it, to seek the
Truth about myself, my world, my life.

I will experience all things intended for me by my Maker
To see and to do, and I will execute them from this chair.
Good. Bad. Wealth. Poverty. Sickness and Health,
My Earthly Heaven, and my Earthly Hell.
My successes, my failures, my all.

After all, if this quest is to be conquered, I can only
Say that without the chair, I can never roll ahead to
Greater achievements.

In closing, ponder this; an empty chair is just a piece of furniture;
There are, however, no limits to the thoughts
That can come from the mind
Of someone sitting
In a piece of
Furniture.

L.E.A.

To A Bottle of Whiskey

Bottle, why do you do this to me? You sit there on my table and I
Imbibe your contents as a man would gulp from a cool stream,
Half dead from thirst.

But I continue to diminish your volume. Its foul fluid
Contaminates my body, its rancid odor impregnates itself on my
Breath 'till I wretch at the smell of it.
I sometimes want to vomit, but even if I did,
My brain is still fogged by the damned liquid.

It is in me, bottle, not in you; but why bother telling you?
You smirk and mock me in my drunken state. And you continue to sit
On my table, in my house.
Bottle...if you had a heart, it would surely be black with sin.
And still you are amused at my inebriated brain and body.
Oh, bottle...I hate you!
with every ounce of contempt I have, I hate you!

Bide your time, bottle; you've not much of it left.
When I sleep tonight you may court my empty glass,
And the ashtray to your right; for they are your allies.

But tomorrow, when dawn breaks, and a new day is again
Born, you will die. I will kill you...break you and shatter you
Into a million fragments. Then, unintoxicated, I will soberly
Sweep your remains into the gutter; where you will find a grave
With your other comrades...all of you empty, and broken, and
Without purpose.

That, bottle, is your destiny. I don't need you. I
Don't want you.
You are not a part of me.

You belong in hell.   *L.E.A.*

The sky so blue
seems to be reflecting
me and you
blossoming in the sun

It makes me happy

You and i grasping our love
as the clouds
holding onto their rainbow
in the sky

It makes me happy

The sweet season of autumn
smothering you and i
in the midst of fallen leaves
Brisk morning, sunny hours

it makes me happy

L.L.

My love for you is calling
just to say i care and
remembering you often
with a special prayer

My love for you is missing you
whenever we're apart
but believing that time will pass
and not what's in my heart

My love for you is deep
filled with joy each day
i hope it never will be such
to turn cloudy or grey

any time would be so right
to tell you how i feel tonight
heh, don't you know
i love you so . . . so much

And my love for you goes beyond
each page
no "mere words" can ever say
what i feel within my heart

L.L.

But there is time
time to find out
who we are
where we're going

time to live
  laugh
  love
and be happy

time to remember those times

Time to learn
and share while learning
to smile and cry
(once in a while)
not like me?

Time to be ourselves

L.L.

Lullabies and bright blue skies
memories in my mind
days of you left behind

  i sit and wait...
  hesitate
  thinking of you

it's been a while
us knowing each other
growing with one another
in our own ways
watching the days
as they pass – so fast

i'm holding you near to me
i feel so close yet so free
all of you is part of me

what must i do to serve you
i ask, let me hear you
you are my heart's delight
with you i feel so right
come sometime and spend the night

L.L.

Don't you know i had a dream last night
and you were here with me
lyin' by my side so soft and warm
and we talked a while and shared a smile
then we shared the dawn
but when i woke up
oh, my dream - it was gone.

Surely you kow how i stand
on the question of my lovin' you
haven't i proved it in so many ways?
more surely than my words can say.

Oh, we're just silly kids
but then again
i've never heard it said
that kids can't fall in love
and feel the same
i can still remember your first
"i love you", Lorraine.

Is this how it's done
or shall i sing and dance
will you give me a chance?
i ask, let me hear you.

Everything is life has a price
will we remain lovers
yes, that would be nice
i'm yours for free
no strings, you see
if you are in love with me.

L.L.

14

Me

The morning are neat
i get dressed and compete
in 8 AM traffic – repeat
4 days a week

It's not the places we're going to
or all the phases
we're going through
What is it that we do.

Who knows what midday brings
Oh – come on,
surprise me
with a day full of lovely things.

Daily changes taking place
in little time
but so much space
it's all ok – i say.

10 PM – a cup of tea
it's just i being me
there's no one else i see.

L.L.

The time is cozing by
and it gets me high
'cause i'm drawing nigh
to you.

Though cells grow and die
in both you and i
i'm still gonna sigh
for you.

You are like a star
in the sky
a smile in my eye
i don't want to say "bye"
to you.

So let me step aside
the tide
awhile and take a ride
with you.

The words i write
i could read all night
but my thoughts
are keeping me high

time is passing by
i'm drawing nigh
to you

L.L.

11 Days After Ten Years

I enjoy seeing the familiar green bug
Drive up.
You step out, effervescent, bubbly, all smiles.
Smiles are nice, Yours are warm.
Warmth is nice, especially if you've been
Cold for a long time.
You're all of these things mixed together
With a very special something thrown in
For good measure.

You're sunshine when it's raining.
You're rain during hot weather - refreshing
Your sweet scents I notice near your
Neck, ears, & wrists.

You're a flower when it's least expected
You're delicate when you choose to be,
Aggressive when you choose to be. Outgoing.
You're a rainbow during sorrow. You are
Never sorrow, sorrowful, or one to "give
It Up."

then there's the missing element, ingredient,
Call it what you will.

I see it when I see you, I see it when
I don't. I can't describe it because it's
Invisible, and therefore intangeable.

I hear it when I hear you, I hear it when
I don't. I can't describe it verbally . . . it
Too is invisible and, therefore intangeable.

I feel it when I feel you, I feel it when
I don't. It too is invisible; intangeable; but
It can be described. So I'll try as best
I can.

The "special thing" that makes you very
Pleasantly different from others is that
Your kiss, your touch, glances, unsaid, but
Understood thoughts, and your uncanny
Understanding make me want to know
As much as I can about you.

I won't say that I'm passionately in love with
You, and I won't say I'm not. It shall
Be left unsaid; left as is.

For now, anyway.

L.E.A.

Images of You

You remind me of Spring –
Fresh, new, sunshine, new life

Yes, cotton is nice
But let it suffice to say
That this poem doesn't rhyme.

I wish I had a beard
For You to groove on, but . . .
Will my chin do?

I liken you to an organizer extraordinaire,
Efficiency expert, and a one in a
Million extra close friend,
Among other things.

V.W's petite things, heart necklaces
Yellow, T-shirts, sensuous perfumes,
Lip gloss, driving all over
Creation, late night conversations about
Love, life, living life to the fullest &
You and me . . . all remind me of you.

Old saying like "super" or "neat oh" or "neat"
Make your overall image unique and complete
                                        Love, Luke

Changes; yet we're still so much the same.
Changes; yet you've still retained your name.
Beauty – you've changed so beautifully, but
                the ink runs dry from my
                pen before I can describe it.
Beauty – A grown-up woman . . . a "new" Lorraine
                that I never knew so intimately
                in the 8th grade in St. Bernadette's
                School.
Beauty – A "Laurie" I've grown to love in less than
6 weeks; because you're so "alive."
Changes – some that can make a body sing,
Changes – some that can take your _soul_ to wing,
They're like a mound of campfire embers,
They're memories I'll always, forever remember.

I'll share them, I'll keep them.
I'll probably someday weep over them.
I don't know. Crying is emotion . . .
Emotion makes me thing of involvement,
                such as a cause . . . and
                with a cause you must
                have devotion.
Ergo . . . my tears of emotion will be "happy" ones,
                tears of joy . . . for _our_
                cause . . . and _your_
                devotion
Changes – some that can make a lady sing,

Changes – some that can take your soul to wing,
They're like a mound of campfire's embers,
They're memories I always, forever remember.

Think of the size of the sky; Please try.
That's how much I'd love to know about you.
the way you look, the way you "are," the way
                you understand those "little
                things," and the way you
                shine like a big yellow
                star!!!
A million miles high, a dot in the sky;
That's you . . . the brilliant yellow star, but
                no matter how far or close
                you are,
You outshine everyone else, just because
                you're the way you are.
Laurie – stay the way you are!

                        L.E.A.

. . . Because I Saw It
(And It Was Beautiful)

I saw the sun this morning, rich, and
Warm, and yellow. And I cried because I saw it.
And it was so beautiful.

I saw a flower this morning, fresh, new
And fragrant. And I cried because I saw it.
And it was so beautiul.

I saw a timepiece this morning, old, yet ticking,
And heard the wonderful sounds of the passage
Of time. Past! Present! Future! And I cried
                    because I saw it.
And it was so beautiful.

I saw the sky, the rain, blue clouds, grey
           clouds, insects, birds,
           pictures, and a hand-
           rubbed wooden bowl.
They were real! Tangeable! Colorful! And I
cried because I saw them.
Yes, they were all real; I did not have to
           imagine them.
And they were so beautiful.

I cried because my tears were ones of joy
For – I saw for so many people who
           have to imagine
           what these things are
           like.
Maybe some day they'll see, and then
I'll cry again . . .
Because it will be so beautiful.

L.E.A.

That's Something
(I'd Truly Like To Be . . .)

I'd like to be a blade of grass,
Or a leaf on a tree,
And have the early morning sun
Shine on me.
That's Something I'd Truly Like To Be.

I'd like to be a fledgling bird, maybe
An eagle would be nice, and very
Regal. If I were a bird, I'd soar
The late blue skies, and try to search,
To know, to learn; to see reality,
That's Something I'd Truly Like To Be.

I'd like to be an antique clock on the wall;
I'd love to see the summers turn to fall
And see the colors of life, of love,
Of these, most of all, life's silent call . . .
That's Something I'd Truly Like To Be.

I'd like to be a fine, wooden guitar
To be played to the Heavens and stars;
And to hear my music make laughter
For young and old, rich and poor, and near and far.
That's Something I'd Truly Like To Be.

I'd like to be a mountain range, many years old
And see all the earth, as high as the sky,
And talk to the earth – and her trees, and her rivers,
And lay across her breast during hot summer suns, and icy, win'try colds.
That's Something I'd Truly Like To Be.

But . . . God made me man,
Just as I am . . . free to learn; to understand,
To live . . . to grow to be a fuller, open-minded man.
Tho' maybe someday I'll learn to use the things God gave
And I'll know life, love, sadness, joy, the laughter
Of a nine year old boy, to share a
Song with those who wish to sing along
In their hearts, or in their souls, let
My song live eons old . . .

I guess I can really be any of these things;
A blade of grass, a soaring bird with outstreched wings,
An antique clock, with a stately "tick-tock" going
On as time passes, I can watch the farmer sew and reap
His oats, and barley, grass and wheat.
And I could be a fine, old guitar, mellowed by the years
Seasoned by a few precious scars, but just as melodious
As a song of Rain, early in the morning – A GIFT
From the stars . . . to remind me.
That I can be – the ideas are more vast than the Seven Seas.

But for now the rain is falling down, singing
My song reminds me of coming down
To Earth, the way it should be all along.
Be creative . . . be an instrument in God's celestial
Orchestra of Heavenly Peace.
Be free, be understanding – Be . . . ME!

(THAT'S ALL THERE IS; YOU SEE!!)

L.E.A.

Some Of The Best Life Has
To Give

A blue sky, tears of joy . . .
Playgrounds full of girls and boys
Fountain pens, a cozy den
A summer night, rainbows, kites . . .
It's some of the best life has to offer.
That's why I really dig this Life I have to live.

Butterflies, a woman's understanding eyes . . .
The radio, my stereo, lis'ning to "Satchmo,"
And any good music; fried eggs and
Sausage links, little trinkets . . .
It's some of the best Life has to offer
Some Of The Best Life Has To Give.

Good movie, free style, poetic license . . .
Poetry, wooden music, a mellow guitar,
All kinds of wood, new-mowed lawns,
Puppies and Nature,
It's more of The Best Life Has To Give,
And that's part of the "WHY?" of why I love the Life
                                                    I live.

Ice cold beer, Southern Comfort twice a year . . .
(New Year's Eve and my birthday),
Yo-yo's, shotting penny-ante craps
A new born baby on my lap . . .
A little more of what's in store ---
And it's some of the best Life has to offer.

A bit of the herb once in a while,
A heartwarming smile;
doing something superbly;
Burning candles after a heavy, wet storm,

Win'try nights when I'm safe; when I'm warm . . .
some more of the things, like when Sinatra sings;
The Best Life Has To Give.
Just a couple more reasons, like the change in the season
Why I wouldn't trade 'ya for another
Life to live.

Remember that smile? An old friend giving a call . . .
Talking a while, sharing that smile, fishing, hunting and thinking.
Pond'ring in a haze about what's beyond . . .
A tiny blue pond with mallard ducks,
Earning badly needed buck,
Just a few more thoughts that I managed to keep from
Being lost, and never caught, to flow from my pen
So, here goes again!
This is the kind of stuff – sometimes tame, sometimes rough,
The Best Life Has To Give . . .
Why write about this Life while I still have the chance?
Because of the wonderful thrills of romance,
Mem'ries of wines, and of evening of dance,
Or a shiny new coin, per chance . . . Either way, I think it's O.K.,

And I'll be doing it all over again today. ---
Lovin' the life;
Lovin' the way; lookin' to find tomorrow today . . .
I'll take snother piece – it seems that it will never cease . . .
It's Some Of The Best Life Has To Give.

THE END

L.E.A.

Tomorrow's sunsets are here today
once i thought days gloomy and grey
but now dismal appearances have gone astray

What has transpired within me?
at long last i've seen
the person i want to be
light – where darkness has been

The radiant sky, the gleam in my eye
so soft and subtle the way
joy are these tears i cry
happiness has crowded my day

L.L.

Mi Corazon

I saw you today, my love, and in spite of all the frustrations
and obligations i have a dream. A dream deeply rooted in my
heart.
      That soon we will see the sun rise and watch it set
as the clouds so blue reflect me and you.
And the rippling waves on the ocean become pleasant memories.
i still have this dream. It lingers . . . in my mind
when i'm awake and not so awake.
I want the warmth of your smile, the gentleness of your heart
      i want to wake up next to you
on the first day of December
after sleeping with you the last day of November.
and we'll be there a while and share a smile - together
      i have this dream
that we're in this together
and the best is yet to come
we've just begun
to live
to love
to laugh
      i need this dream
you make me feel that anything is possible
i wake up with a smile that only you can comprehend
my love, my friend
      i have this dream . . . that some day we will build
on the foundation i believe we started today.
And my whole being wants to shout
i care
i love
i want
i need

But , it's difficult – this dream. I can't do it alone.
It's easier to care and to love than to say i need and i want -
i must be careful.
You see, in this need, with this dream to want, to care, to
love you, i must be careful. i may wait too long
for days that will not come or i may treasure shortlived hopes.

Te quiero mas que a nadie

L.L.

Sitting on 2nd Avenue

i grab my keys
pick up my sack
books neatly packed
hurriedly, i rush to class
dreaming of you
and Second Avenue.

"Hello – how are you."
"Fine, who me?
I'll have that pacer
welded by three."

Great – 5 more minutes
they will quickly pass
one short break, then
my final class

Heh little lady
been busy today
what good came your way?
Got an A on a test
by the way.

Gotta run now
I'll see you at 8
If I'm not there please wait
Sure I will, I have no date.

Yes, Dr. Primack
I so agree
please define "reality"
Bring your papers
don't be late

We'll finish this
on Friday's date.

The leaves have fallen
as I walk passed
Alachua General
at long last – I see
my VW and me
heading back to #5C

The phone is ringing
as I'm singing
"Heh Love
How you be?"
"Fine. Want company?
    See you Thursday
        just about 3."

L.L.

Five Days After Two Months

On September eleventh
i left and you came with me
for a while
both of us beginning – what is new
and end of old lives
starting anew . . . together
(me and you)

Sharing weekends with you
And during weekdays
dreaming . . . of Friday evenings
You sitting at your desk
at 3807 – i'm in heaven
falling in love (again) with crazy you
catching planes
and
occasional strains of
a cold once in a while

Month #3 is approaching
i long to be together (with you)
in the am, lyin' by my side
late at night asking me
if i want to make love
(it's so good)
next to me when i'm sleeping
i feel your warm body
close to me – if i should cry
your beautiful hands
touch my tiny face
you embrace me with
soft caresses and sweet kisses

We have learned to break away
from those things we
previously – held on to –
lifestyles we no longer need
and it's so different now
and in between
all this time and space
i believe you
and i want you . . . in all the ways
there are to want

In the winter
with the cool breeze and
my mid-morning sneeze
i long for you
and when spring draws near
will you still be here
so we can continue
for as long as
I hope the 11th of September will be back
and come again and again.

L.L.

God Bless The Seed

God, bless and keep the seeds for all
Of time,

For within the seed there is life,
Waiting to be given the right Time,
Circumstances, and love to grow,
And to prosper.

From the seed comes food, and drink and
All of Nature's raw materials that
Touch our lives.
Every day of every week of every year.

But most of all, God, bless the
Seeds of life;
Those that will be fertilized,
And grow into strong, understanding young men and women.
Because their's is the seed of tomorrow . . . the hopes
And dreams of the future.

Bless their seed, and protect them,
For without them there is not hope.
Without the seed there is nothing.

Please, God, bless the seed.

THE END
L.E.A.

At Sunset

At sunset, when most of the cars and trains and
Noisey modes of transport have reached their destination,
I am most at peace with myself.

At sunset, it is peaceful, tranquil, and serene;
A time for recollection, and reflection.

The whole world takes time to yawn, and to stretch,
And to get ready for sleep.

It's a time to talk to God . . . however you perceive Him.
The owl stirs, in preparation for the night of hunting
The Heavens light up, and the stars twinkle.
The world is at rest.

And the children . . . ah, the children. They are saying
Their prayers, asking for a drink of water, and
Kissing the dog or cat good night.
They are happy.

Tired from play, and bellies full from
Supper, they fall into slumber
With the promise of another day
Just around the bend in their dreams.

L.E.A.

Wedding

You are now, in the eyes of God
Joined as one for the rest of your
      lives.
It is perhaps, one of the most beautiful
        and sacred things on Earth.
If nothing else, remember this: the
        love which you professed
To each other is the strongest force in
        the universe. It can
And will overcome that which seems
        to be the most insur-
        mountable obstacles you
Will encounter throughout your lives,
Share, confess, and be yourselves;
For it is in this honesty that you
        will conquer the
Smallest, and the most turbulent
        crises in your life
        together.
May God be with you, and bless
        all that you experience,
Or dream of; and, ultimately achieve
        together. And always

Remember, with Him, your love can
only grow stronger, for it
Was love, and the desire to nurture &
strengthen that love
That realized this Holy Union.

Be open, be free and above all, be
committed to each other.
God will take care of all else.

L.E.A.

Outdoorsman

Who else can so fully appreciate the absolute
                beauty of nature than the
                outdoorsman?
Perhaps the relaxation is in sitting apart
                from the rest of the world,
Rod and reel in hand, as you watch the
                birth of a new day.
A gentle breeze blows over the water, and
                rocks the boat so slightly,
Almost hypnotically. The march hens and rails
                the grackles all begin to stir.
And now you see streaks of brilliant orange
                and yellow stretching far off
On the horizon, like endlessly long fingers of some unknown entity.
Dragonflies skitter overhead, and each claims
                the top of a cattail as it's
Own, then takes to the air again.
Far off in the distance, just to the left is a
                wooden area, the beginning of
A great forest of hundreds of trees, plants and
                animals.
All manner of creature, from the tiny spidermite
                to the awsome wild bear
Can be found there, each wanting nothing more
                than to live out their lives,
                and perpetuate the species.
You know this, for you have been there,
                and marveled at many things
                within their domain.
Dew drops on an oil web, glistening like pear
                in the early morning sun,

Or the pair of thrushes bringing morsel after
                morsel to the gaping mouths
                inside the nest.
The otters, whose main concern seemed to be
                to play and cavort from your
                sole enjoyment.
Though civilization may be a mile away, or a
                hundred, to be able to seek
Out these beautiful times and bear witness to
                them is indeed something special.
Few are the men who realize these wonders
                and respect them, however
Insignificant they might seem, then return
                home with the inner
Peace of one who knows not only his worth,
                but also that of the world
                around him.

L.E.A.

Courage

What makes the clouds to form different shapes?
What makes the wine to come out of the grapes?
What's the real secret beneath Batman's cape?
        Courage.
What drives the camel to carry his load?
What put our friend the fork in the road?
What makes a dynamite stick to explode?
        Courage
What, in the dark of the dreariest night
Beckons the millions of stars to stay bright?
What makes the fireflies light up their lights?
What makes a prizefighter step in and fight?
What makes the complex computer compute?
What makes the fluetist to flaunt on his flute?
What makes the shootist to take aim and shoot?
        Courage.
What makes the salmon to swim back upstream?
What makes people change from their brand to Gleem?
What makes the dreamers dream beautiful dreams?
        Courage.
What makes the skier search out the steep slopes?
What makes the hangman to pull on the rope?
And who put the ant into antelope?
        Courage.
Who, in a furious moment of rage
Wrote down the thoughts on the poet's blank page?
Then stalked the great cats, and soon had them caged?
        Courage.

What makes an athlete run a great race?
What makes a man throw a pie in the face?
And who put the steeple in Steeplechase?
                    Courage.
What makes a man to become a great King?
What makes Pavarotti stand up and sing?
What makes a man give a woman a ring?
                    Courage.
What makes a Timex much more than a watch?
And who puts the butter in Butterscotch?
Look deep enough, and you'll find we've All got
                    Courage.

L.E.A.

FOR ALL OF THOSE WHO WEAR THE WHITE

For all of those who wear the white;
And care for us both day and night.
While listening to our grunts and groans;
Of bedpans full of fresh gallstones.
For those of you who check I.V.'s;
And tend to post-cystoscopies.
I put my thoughts down into verse;
For every aide and every nurse.

I know it seems I sometimes ring;
For some inconsequential things.
But in the bitter moments I have tasted;
Your acts of love are never wasted.
And those poor souls who miss that fact;
Are ignorant, or else they lack
That inner spark which lights the Soul;
and makes a human being whole.

For all of you who know so well;
Your patient's feeling living hell.
And only by syringe or pill
that mystic sleep will make him still.

With every once of mustered might;
You tend our wants, however trite.
And when at last your shift is done;
The war goes on but the battle's won.

And some of you will keep in mind;
A few of us you've left behind.
And on the morrow, as you toil;
I hope the memories are sweet, not spoiled.
For some of us you were the rock;
On whom we leaned through those rough spots.
And when, once or twice, I broke and cried;
You soothed my soul and dried my eyes.

For all of you who wear the white;
I penned these words because they're right.
It's you who are His chosen ones;
To heal His daughter and His sons.
Applaud yourselves and hone your skills;
And please keep strengthening our wills.

L.E.A.

A Very Special
New Year's Day
Recipe

~ Preparations ~

Start with a clean, fresh,
wide open heart, open to new ideas.
This can best be accomplished through
a few quiet moments of prayer,
meditation, or reflection.

~ Ingredients ~

One large portion of the joy of living,
however humble.
One large seasoned helping of under-
standing for all people – everywhere.
A touch of humility
A generous sprinkling of humor
Several parts joy, sorrow, love,
trust, lost love, mistrust, surprise &
doubt. (Anticipation will add a un-
ique flavor as well).

~Directions ~

Into clear, fresh heart, read each
of ingredients, then slowly, thor-
oughly mix and feel them until they

are completely absorbed, understood
& accepted. Warm slowly with the
spark of the indominable human spirit,
Then bring to boil with the fire of
every human emotion at it's zenith.
Cook with the chill of a brisk winter
breeze.

~ Serving Suggestions ~

Serve as needed, using your own
discretion. Let the heart be your guide.
Note – In certain instances a
small portion will be more than enough;
in other instances, the larger the portion,
the better!

Yield – Approximately 365 days. Then
repeat recipe.

L.E.A.

DAVID

THE BUBBLE BOY IN TEXAS, WHOS NAME WAS DAVID DIED TODAY.
AND THOUGH I NEVER KNEW HIM, THERE'S SOME THINGS I'D LIKE TO SAY.

THE LITTLE BOY WAS ONLY TWELVE; HE COULD'VE BEEN MY SON,
AND EVEN THOUGH HE WASN'T, THERE WAS TOO MUCH LEFT UNDONE.

YOU SEE, HE NEVER RODE A TWO WHEEL BIKE WITH HIS FRIENDS
ALONG THE STREET, AND NOT A SINGLE DROP OF OCEAN WATER EVER
TOUCHED YOUNG DAVID'S FEET.

I GUESS HE NEVER RODE A HORSE, OR EVEN RAN A RACE, OR SAILED OUT
ON THE OCEAN BLUE WITH SEA SPRAY ON HIS FACE.

HE NEVER HIT A HOMERUN ONCE, OR CAUGHT A TOUCHDOWN PASS
OR PRAYED BEFORE A SEDER, OR CELEBRATED MASS. HE NEVER GOT TO
BRING THINGS INTO SCHOOL FOR SHOW AND TELL. AND I DOUBT HE EVER
TOSSED A COIN INTO A DEEP OLD WISHING WELL.

HE NEVER HELD A BUTTERFLY, OR SKIPPED ROCKS THAT WENT "KER-PLUNK!"

HE NEVER CAMPED OUT 'NEATH THE STARS, SO HE NEVER SMELLED A SKUNK.

FERRIS WHEELS, BLUE WINGED TEALS, AND HAY RIDES-HE MISSED ALL.

HE NEVER HELD A GARTER SNAKE OR AN INFANT OH SO SMALL.

THE ONE THING, THOUGH, I KNOW HE HAD, WAS HIS BIG WHITE COWBOY
HAT. AND DREAMS OF SOMEDAY BEING WHERE OTHER COWBOYS MIGHT BE
AT.

HE NEVER FLEW A KITE SO BRIGHT, SO HIGH UP IN THE SKY.

HE NEVER DID SO MANY THINGS BUT, WAIT FRIENDS. . . .
LETS NOT CRY.

I'M SURE, THOUGH, DAVID 'ERE YOU ARE THAT YOU CAN SURELY SEE
THE SUN WILL SOON BE COMING UP AND
DAVID---NOW YOU'RE FREE.

L.E.A.

48

Love Thoughts

Though my body's somewhat twisted, and I'm
Pretty sure I missed it when the good Lord
Gave out stamina and speed,
I'm quite confident in knowing that through all
My years of growing, in my heart He gave me
All the love I need.

I can't fully yet explain it, but there's something
In my brain that says it's much more fun to give
Than to receive.
And the love that's in the giving lights the faces of
The living
And it makes me glad to see what I've
Achieved.

To kiss an infant, smell a flower, see a
Rainbow, hold a woman, or to watch
A newborn day to come alive,
Reaffirms when I am down, that there is
Love all around me,
I am that spark within my soul that seems
To survive.

If this seems too optimistic or appears
so unrealistic, if it sounds as if my
Recipe is wrong.
Look around you – stop and listen, touch
A morning dew drop glistening,

Hear the voice of God in ev'ry
Creature's song.

For you see, love holds a power that, at any
Given hour, can heal a body, soul, or mind or
Broken heart.
But that power needs a chance, like the
Loving good-bye glance that two lovers
Give each other as they part.

They know deep within their breast and neither
Lover can contest that even temporarily apart
Each feels alone.
And when at last they're reunited, all their
Unrequited love flows through their souls
Clear to the morrow of their bones.

My pen is growing dry now, and few other
Thoughts have I, now that this verse of love
I've written is all done.
And the thing we must remember is that
Love is like an ember burning deep
Within the hearts of everyone.

L.E.A.

In my routine, organized daily grind
Alone at night, i sit and unwind
the day is gone the evening is here
i often wonder as tomorrow draws near

Often to sleep i lie awake
my slumber being to dream i take
as thoughts wander to hours passed
my magical dream i try to cast
then the moring and the alarm rings
Another day of the same, old thing!

L.L.

Our love, i thought, it would grow
with hope and promise as you know
But then one day it came to end
And my heart, it took long to mend

Four years later i still miss you so
for reasons, selfish, i do know
My life is happy in ways but some
i've much to offer and have no one

the early days i thought would flourish
But in their stead became less porous
i picked up the pieces got on with life
getting accustomed to all but being a wife

it's funny now how life it seems
can be incomplete, a shattered dream
We're all here for some unknown reason
Every time and place, are the seasons

someday i'd like to talk and smile
to sit with you for just a while
reminiscing only all the good times
over a splendid dinner and a glass of wine   *L.L.*

Past

As days go by i wonder why
my heart is heavy and i sigh
the world full of hope it seems
but why, i ask, can't my dream
that often has my daily thought
became a past of all that's not

i vascillate between now and then
When bliss, it seemed, had no end
And as i sit my hand with pen
i ask myself if i can lend
Another day of this old scene
or apt, in haste, for my <u>magical</u> dream.

L.L.

i want some things taken for granted
like small children and flowers planted
day after day my life is the same
a successful career and no more to gain
The clock ticks away – I've much to do
my magical dream, could it include you?

L.L.

Truly, i apologize for the (often) times i
am obstinate and sarcastic. Frequently, it helps . . .
in a world full of disillusion. But, i am
enamored with hope for love, for peace, and
the challenge to make a difference.
My soul aches but my heart is full. The humor i
portray is not false – truly i have a "joie de
vivre" and much sentiment in my entire being.
My weaknesses are many; however, my strengths
are not encumbered by them.
And, it is those i wish to portray . . . in my
personal and professional lives.
i don't want the initial impression, i have
(had) of you, tainted. Therefore, i think you
should concentrate on YOU and those things
you excel at – and, i – me, and neither of us
will be disappointed. i may "when i am an
old woman" laugh or cry – or both. But, in the
end, i will have survived and, at a minimum,
touched someone's heart the way i yearn for
mine to be captured.
God is good and He's been good to me. i feel
blessed and, in numerous ways, special.
i know He won't let me down. but, i have to
do my part and, i haven't really discovered
what that is. i know what i want but not
how to go after it. Why does life have to
be so complicated? Perhaps it's because
we lend a hand in the process.
Be true to yourself. Go after your
dreams. And, in the meantime, if our paths
should again cross, i'll always remember
the laughter.

L.L.

The Magic of
"It's a Wonderful Life"

Christmastime – oh, what a time – a special, magical
time of year!
A time for joy and peace and love – a time for joyful
tears.
And on T.V.'s around the world – East and West and to
both poles
That magic film, "It's a Wonderful Life."
Will warm ten million souls.

It's the story of George Baily – Good hearted, small
town, family man
And how, that snowy freezing Christmas Eve
He felt his world falling through his hands.

He's so distraught, confused and scared,
He knows not where to turn.
He's lost his faith, and most all hope;
His heart's fire barely burns.

"George, you're worth more dead than alive,"
Chides the richest, meanest man in town.
So George runs to a bridge down the road
And cautiously looks down.

Of course, we know he doesn't jump, and all's
fine in the end.
But George is shown some strange new sights,
He has no life! No friends!

It's like a videocassette of life with no George
Bailey there.
So many things, so wrong, so sad,
It gives George quite a scare.

For me to say what happens next
Would simply not be fair.
Suffice to say that what George Bailey sees is
More than he can bear.

But enough of the story and characters now,
Already too much I have told you.
See for yourself, "It's a Wonderful Life,"
Let it entrance, delight and enfold you.

You see, there really <u>is</u> magic in those celluloid
                    strips,
In the dialogue, the actors, the sets.
There are subtleties woven all throughout the tale
It's just something you never forget.

Very briefly, in closing , one though overwhelms me
As tears of joy roll down my cheek:
It's a shame we can't <u>all</u> live in Bedford Falls . . .
With the Capra and Stewart mystique.

L.E.A.

My Gratitude Journal –
A Continuance

Saturday
July 25th, 1998

1) I'm thankful for (three-way)
conference calling, and for people
who call back after my leaving
a message.

2) I'm thankful for friends who
give you their BEST advice when
asked . . . and truly mean it.

3) I am thankful for "snacks."

4) I'm thankful for calligraphy,
and surprise letters.

5) I'm thankful for finding an
old movie classic/classic movie
while (I'm) channel surfing!

Sunday
July 26th, 1998

1) Im thankful for naps they refresh
the body, leave us "unable" to
worry about the day-to-day, hour-
to-
hour problems, choices, and, some-
times
difficult decisons which face us all.

2) I'm thankful for lounging
around, brunch, and TOTALLY re-
laxing (no matter HOW you choose to) on
Sundays.

3) I'm thankful for the show "60
Minutes," ESPECIALLY Andy Rooney!

4) I'm thankful for that strange, ex-
hilarating feeling that preceeds going
someplace "special" . . . especially
when it's somewhere I've never
been, and something I've never done.

5) I'm thankful for 'next-day-shipp-
ing.'

Monday,
July 27th, 1998

1) I am thankful for
people who are punctual, for they
understand that not only is my
time valuable (and is so showing respect
for that), but so is THEIRS . . . I like that

2) I'm thankful for surprise phone
calls from family members and
friends.

3) I'm thankful for the "Headlines"
segment on the Tonight Show w/ Jay Leno.

4) I'm thankful for serendipitous things.

5) I'm thankful for people who go
out of their way, especially in busi-
ness, to work with you when you
are either on a limited budget or
can't decide EXACTLY what you
want. (The WHOLE WORLD needs more
people like them!)

Tuesday,
July 28th, 1998

1) I am thankful for good "B.C.D.'S."

2) I'm thankful for people who
understand my little quirkes & idio-
syncrasies.

3) I'm thankful for being able to
see small wild creatures through
my window from my bed.
4) I'm thankful for Munster cheese!

5) I'm thankful for people who care
about me – and TELL ME SO!

Wednesday,
July 29th, 1998

1) I am thankful for great naps
as the rain falls to earth; it's
as if the Angels are crying tears of
joy.

2) I am thankful for surprise phone calls from family and friends MOST ESPECIALLY ROSEY!!! ☺

3) I am thankful for the AOL Instant Messenger.

4) I am thankful for FX's "The Collectables" show; and "The Super Collectors" show.

5) I am thankful for the return (seeing him again) of the Gecko who lives outside my apartment, over the automatic door.

Thursday,
July 30th, 1998

1) I am thankful for the Simpsons @ 6:30 P.M.

2) I am thankful for clean fresh-smelling laundry.

3) I'm thankful for the "Card-O-Matic"
computerized laundry/washing system.

4) I am thankful for my shower-wheelchair.

5) I am VERY thankful for Rosey
Anne Marie being so damned UNDER-
STAND[ING] regarding me, <u>ESPECIALLY</u> . . .
"WANNA BUY A WATCH?!?!?!?"

Friday,
July 31st, 1998

1) I am thankful that people confide
in me – especially Robyn, who
for her short 16 years has endured
so much hell yet is willing to
"let me into" her "NEW" world. I
wish her only good things. God,
please bless this special young woman.

2) I am always thankful for weekends

3) I am thankful for serendipitous con-
versations with my Griffin Avenue
neighbors

3) I am thankful that I finally "know"
my cousin Jeanette H. Smith.

4) I am VERY THANKFUL for caller I.D.
and the Bell South calling/home telephone
plan(s).

5) I AM THANKFUL FOR BEING ABLE
TO WRITE, "I'M THANKFUL."

Saturday,
August 1st, 1998

1) I am thankful for every blessing, (no
matter how large or small), that God
granted me during the month of July

2) I am thankful when I hear things are
going well for family, and, (in
a different, but wholly special,
"corrected" way) my friends.

3) I am thankful for the privilege
of volunteering @ the Animal Control
Centers; (especially when we "match"
people w/pets, or reunite them!)

4) I am thankful for SST drivers who
KNOW WHERE THE CIR destination is!

5) I am thankful for being able to
sleep late tomorrow (and stay up LATE
tonight).

Sunday 8-2-98

1) I am thankful for Sunday brunches,
with coffee, and bagel perhaps, a ba-
nana (or a slice of cantaloupe) This
followed by a waffle, or maybe a
cinnamon Bun! Ohhhh, Sundays! ☺

2) I am thankful for the "Wedding Story" series, and I wish all of the couples who got married on the program, as well as those who will in the future nothing but health, happiness and all the gifts God chooses to bestow on them, especially healthy children!

3) I am thankful for the television show, "Touched By An Angel" . . . (I know/believe/am sure that I have been – many times throughout my life)

4) I am equally thankful when, after the lyric is written (as I usually do 1st), the music just "appears" in my mind; and as I pick up my guitar, it's almost as if my hands "know" where to go and what strings and frets must be used.

Monday,
August 3rd, 1998

1) I am thankful for the ability to enjoy ORGANIZED CHAOS – (like my apartment!)
2) I am thankful for NEW guitar strings.

3) I'm thankful for Mira; she is, I TRULY BELIEVE, one of my Guardian Angels.

4) I am thankful for "mini" T.V. film festivals, like Bogart week, Tracy/ Hepburn week, etc.)

5) I'm thankful for being able to do fairly decent impressions. For me, it's an incredible stress reliever, and I thank God for it.

L.E.A.

i'm full of life
take some of mine
we'll both grow
in space and time
won't you be a friend of mine?

i've much to give –
to offer you
won't you take my heart
we'll both grow together
now's the time to start

so, as i write this poetry
(a little thing)
to you from me
i think thoughts – very kind
(won't you be a friend of mine?)

L.L.

Surely you know
how i stand
on the question of my lovin' you
haven't i proved it
in so many ways
more surely than my words
can say

Oh, we're just silly kids
but then again
i've never heard it said
that kids can't fall in love
and feel the same
i can still remember
your first "i love you lorraine"

Is this how it's done
or shall i sing and dance
will you give me a chance?
i ask – let me hear you

Everything in life has a price
will we remain lovers
heh, that would be nice
i'm yours for free
no strings you see
if you are in love with me!

L.L.

I Saw A Stranger

I saw him in the park one day; it was early in November.
I guess he must've been about seventy-five, if not eighty, and
I happened to look at him, and he at me for an instant. His
whole life seemed to unfold before me in that brief, fleeting
moment. I think that he must have surely done everything, seen
everything, and then some. I would have bet that he'd seen many
a snow-capped mountain – perhaps even climbed a few himself,
and I wondered how many times the old man had watched the seasons
change from winter to spring to summer to fall. I thought about
the children he had, and of their children, and, maybe even
their's again. How many things had the old man taught his children
and grandchildren? How many runny noses had he cleaned? And how
many bruised knees and elbows had those eyes seen and patched up
with a few band-aids here and there, and a kiss or a pat on the
back? And then, of course, there were the Christmases...ah! the
tree with all the trimmings, and the stockings hung from the
mantle above the fireplace that the old man himself had built
way back in the early thirties. And we can't forget all the
Thanksgivings, also with everything from soup to nuts. Each,
it seemed, was more glorious and more celebrated than the last.

Then, sort of falling into some king of irreversible pat-
tern, the old man's children all managed to move away, taking
with them their children. Why? I haven't a single idea, nor, does
it seem, does the old man.

Maybe that's why he comes to the park and feeds the pigeons,
and just watches life going by. And that's such a shame; there's
so much more to do than play checkers with the other old men

All in all though, as saddening as it is, seeing him just sitting there feeding the pigeons who look upon him as friend and provider, I think I learned something. It's a hard thing to write on paper, but it's very easy to feel when you're there. The feeling humbles a soul, and you almost want to cry, and maybe you do; and you also want to laugh, shout, run, jump, dance, and, maybe even pray. And maybe you do.

L.E.A.

Can There Be A Better Way?
(words and music by L. Angelastro)
(Am, F, G, C, for guitar)

Dark black curtains all around,
Greystone walls from the ground,
Income tax deadline the 15th of May . . .
Can there be a better way?
Can there be a better way?

Hammer and sickle in the Eastern world reigns,
Fills everyone with it's torture and pains;
It's an earthly hell from day to day . . .
Can there be a better way?
Can there be a better way?

Now listen to me people; I've got something to say:
God's purpose for us here is to live for today;
To help one-another and all mankind-
Each individual's identity to find.
But with rocket and warhead we destroy one-another;
Despite God's plan of treating all as a brother.
(music)
So as I leave you with this thought,
Remember the words "What Hath God Wrought?"
Live these words as you live each day,
And perhaps someday there'll be a better way.
(Fads out repeating last line)

THE END

Young Man, Old Man

Rain; sometimes it can be very depressing, as on this mid-July morning. A light mist fell as I looked out at the sky. The weatherman had said rain, and, from the looks of the sky, it wasn't going to stop anytime soon. So what was I doing out on a day like this? Thinking. It was my day off, and I felt as if I HAD to get out of the house, or I'd start climbing the walls. I had chosen to come to the local park to do my thinking; partly because I like the seclusion that was inevitable at this time of the day, and partly because I felt at ease here. I guess it was the atmosphere. I don't really know. Anyway, I wanted to do some serious thinking about a few things that had been on my mind for a long time. Things that I couldn't approach with the right attitude at home, or at the office. Basically, what was on my mind was this: I'm at a time in my life when I have to start to make some very serious decisions. No, not just what to eat and when, but what am I going to be doing in, say, three years? Or five? How am I going to ride this big merry-go-round that we call life? The rain was still drizzling down on me, and I began to wonder whether or not I should have stayed in bed, and thought my great philosophical thoughts some other day. Then I saw the old man. He was sitting on a park bench, with an old newspaper, part of which he was reading, and part of which he was using to cover himself from the rain. The old man was wearing what looked to be an old, worn out Homburg, which was a size or so too large, thereby giving him the appearance of a little boy, from far away. As I drew closer, I could see him better; though I know I'd probably cry later. (I'm very sentimental.) The old man was chewing on what was left of an apple, and seemed not to notice me as I started to think about him, and whether or not he ever took a walk on a rainy morning to think about his future. Suddenly it all became very clear – and very sad. I began to

wonder how many Julys the old man had seen in his years, and why he was
here now, on this dismal morning, and all alone. Where was his family?
Where were his friends? Did he even have any? I began to think of just
how many seasons the old man had seen. How many Julys? Fifty? Sixty-five?
Seventy? I had not the slightest idea, except that he must have seen
plenty of wonderful things in his time, and probaby some that weren't so
wonderful.

    I could see his face now, and it was a sad face indeed. The years
had etched and carved thick lines and crevices into his face. The seasons
had weathered and worn his face and hands, though I knew that he must
have once had a handsome face, and hands like those of an artist, or
a craftsman.

    How many toys had he made for his children? And their children?
And how many Christmases did he share with his family that I was suddenly
and inexplicable thinking about ? Was he the one who, by tradition, always
carved the turkey at Thanksgiving? And did he say the blessing before
the family sat back and enjoyed the feast, after telling stories and
making snowmen with carrot noses and charcoal eyes? Was he the one who
lit the fireplace so that all could gather around, and be enveloped by
its warmth? I tried to imagine him sitting with his grandchildren,
roasting marshmallows and popping popcorn, while the snow mounted in
little hills on the window panes.

    The rain was coming down harder now, and the old man was getting up.
He started walking toward me, and I halfway turned around, so it wouldn't
look like I was staring. I really didn't want to appear rude.

    As the old man passed by me, I caught a glimpse of his eyes. They were
big wide eyes, and they were gray. There was a cataract on the left one;
I saw it when he raised his head in order that he could see where he was
going. The old man looked at me for a split instant, as if to say hello,
and I sort of ackowledged him with a little nod. This he saw, and, to

my suprise, walked up to me, and said, "Young man, what are you doing out in the rain like this? You're apt to catch your death of cold!"

Not wanting to say that I was spying on him, (was I really)? I said that I had come here to think. (That wasn't a lie.) "I like to walk and think," I said. "It's very relaxing for me; only I hadn't counted on the rain," (I lied again.) The old man smiled and without the slightest hint of hesitation, said "C'mon young man, let's have a hot cup of coffee. I know a place that serves the best coffee in town – all you can drink for 50¢. How about it?"

By now I was almost as cold as I was wet, and I wasted no time saying yes to the old man, though I didn't know him from Adam. But I did know that he had a certain – something. And he wanted to share it. That was plain to see.

In ten minutes we were sitting at a coffee shop counter a few blocks away, and while we warmed ourselves with the delicious liquid, the old man told me his story.

"...And that's why I come here to think," he said as he swallowed the last of his third cup of coffee. "Reminds me of all I have to be thankful for, 'ya know. I think that's the problem with most people today; they don't know how to just get up, get out, and enjoy the things that are really important: the feel of a summer rain, the sunrise and sunset, things like that. Seems like people today are too caught up in themselves to care 'bout their fellow man. I don't know–that's just an old man's opinion, but I've been around a long time, and I still get just as much of a kick now as I did when I was a kid. And this park wasn't even built yet.

"Yes, indeed – I love to come here and think of all the old times my family and I used to have. Why, I remember the holidays...we used to all sit around the fireplace and drink hot chocolate and toast marsh-mallows after we came in from playing in the snow. Then, when the smell of the Thanksgiving turkey was so good that you thought you couldn't wait,

Mom would call me to carve it up for us. Oh, yes – and the Christmases...
I used to love to watch the children open their presents on Christmas
morning. Sometimes we even made presents for each other..." He stopped
long enough to sigh, and to smile.

I finished my cup of coffee, and started to reach for the check.
"Oh no," said the old man. "This was on me. Now, why did you say you
were out there this morning?" the old man asked, as he replaces his Hom-
burg.

I collected my thoughts. "Well," I began. "I came to think...to find
some answers, but I think I've found all the answers I'll be needing for
a while."

THE END
L.E.A.

Chains

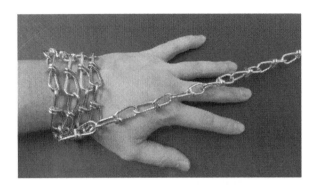

A chain . . .
Symbol of all that binds . . . and holds us captive.

There are chains of steel . . . solidly linked . . .
seemingly unbreakable . . . chains that can shackle our
arms and legs . . . holding us in physical bondage.

    Still other chains . . . stranger and harsher . . .
grip our minds and spirits . . . locking them in fear . . .
shackling us from within . . . sometimes with our consent . . .
most often against our will.

    More vicious chains ring us round . . . in a
tightening circle of poverty . . . prejudice . . . disease
. . . exploitation . . . social bands that cripple
the spirit . . . restrict creativity . . . and
hinder growth.

    Daily experience reveals our bongage . . .
the evening news reports it . . . We are all
enslaved . . . by chains we are helpless to break.

L.E.A.

How sad it would be if there were no more whales,
With their great salty spouts and incredible tails
Those huge graceful bodies sometimes 50 feet long
Their warm gentle ways and their beautiful songs.
And what of giraffes, so slender and tall?
And think of the zebras and hamsters so small.
No more butterflies to signal the spring.
Their dazzling colors on opulent wings.
No more fishes to tug at a boy's first cane pole
No more crecets or frogs in the old swimming hole.
Sad too, it would be if there were no more birds
No more eagles or hawks, only mem'ries and words.
No more sparrows, or sea gulls, or card'nils or jays
Screeching raucous hosannas in their loud, boisterous
ways.
And don't forget rabbits, and mule deer and bears
Or antelope, foxes, and snakes, if you dare!
A world with no pandas, and the elephant's gone
When the snow leopard's cry is a now extinct song.
And still we continue to foul the land,
With sewage in rivers, toxic waste on the sand.
And still we keep cutting down acres of trees
Destroying the homes of creatures like these.
Are we that self centered? Is it that we don't care?
It's not just our planet, it's our planet to share.

L.E.A.

Acknowledgments

First and foremost, to my parents who recognized the value of education. I believe the basics I learned in Catholic school gave me the foundation needed to achieve and excel. The Sisters, who gave their lives to serve others, instilled in me a love of writing, reading and learning. I thank them from the bottom of my heart.

To Christine Keleny of CKBooks Publishing, this is our second collaboration. Christine does all of the behind the scenes work that the reader does not see. She is always responsive, professional and helpful and I recommend her to anyone thinking about self-publishing. And to Kari Ley of Leyout Solutions for creating and designing my book cover. She took my vision and made it come to life.

Images in order of appearance

the things i like   https://pixabay.com/users/wokandapix-614097/

On Thinking of the World   https://pixabay.com/users/public-domainpictures-14/

Don't you know I had a dream   https://pixabay.com/users/bil-jast-2868488/

11 days After Ten Years   https://pixabay.com/users/jaymant-ri-362084/

Because I Saw It   https://pixabay.com/users/suwit_luangpipat-sorn-6294786/

Mi Corazon   https://pixabay.com/users/pexels-2286921/

God Bless The Seed   https://pixabay.com/users/kirillslov-8058952/

Wedding   https://pixabay.com/users/stocksnap-894430/

FOR ALL THOSE WHO WEAR THE WHITE   https://www.pexels.com/photo/group-of-medical-students-at-the-hall-way-3985149/

A Very Special New Year's Day   https://pixabay.com/users/photos-foryou-124319/

Our love, i thought, it would grow   https://pixabay.com/users/go-ranh-3989449/the

The Magic of "It's a Wonderful Life"   https://pixabay.com/users/jamesdemers-3416

A Different Kind of Chair   https://pixabay.com/users/feroban-jo-22932/

I Saw A Stranger https://pixabay.com/users/sharonang-99559

Chains   https://pixabay.com/users/jsgarnerauthor-4294116

—

About the Authors

Laurie Luongo was born in Boston and lived in Somerville, MA until her family relocated to Florida. She is a graduate of the University of Florida and holds a lifetime certification as a Senior Professional in Human Resources. Her career spanned over four decades in hotels and hospitals. She currently advocates for nursing home reform in memory of her mother. She is working on her second non-fiction book about America's loss of civility and what must be done to get it back.

Lucas Angelastro was born in New York. His family moved to Florida when he was a young boy because of his medical issues. Luke was a lover of nature and a collector, particularly of coins. He taught himself to play the guitar and was gifted at song-writing, poetry and prose. He became a paraplegic as a teenager and resided in Florida until his untimely death in 2002. The writings in this book appear exactly as he wrote them beginning in the 1970s.

Made in the USA
Monee, IL
14 February 2022

90475511R00052